Bach Lute Suites
for Guitar

Edited and Fingered by
Jerry Willard

THE MUSIC EMPORIUM
2018 MASSACHUSETTS AVENUE
CAMBRIDGE, MASSACHUSETTS 02140

Ariel Publications
New York · London · Tokyo · Sydney · Cologne

Acknowledgements

I am deeply indebted to Laura Lessard, George Glock,
and Marcel Robinson, whose scholarly work helped to
make this book possible. I am particularly indebted to
J. S. Bach, without whose compositions this book would
have been impossible.

Edited by Peter Pickow
Cover design by Nina Clayton

e d c b a

International Standard Book Number: 0-8256-9979-7

Distributed throughout the world by Music Sales Corporation:
33 West 60th Street, New York 10023
78 Newman Street, London W1P 3LA
2-13-19 Akasaka, Tamondo Bldg., Minato-ku, Tokyo 107
27 Clarendon Street, Artarmon, Sydney NSW 2064
Kölner Strasse 199, D-5000, Cologne 90

Contents

Introduction

Johann Sebastian Bach composed for the lute throughout most of his life. The First Lute Suite was composed in Weimar (1708-1723), the Fourth Lute Suite, the Prelude in C minor and the Fuge in G minor in Cöthen (1717-1723), the Second Lute Suite, the Third Lute Suite, and the Prelude, Fuge, and Allegro in Leipzig (1723-1750). Bach also wrote specifically for the lute in an aria in the Saint John Passion and in a recitative in the Funeral Music for Queen Christiane Eberhardine. We know that Bach was a good friend of the great German lutenist Silvius Leopold Weiss and established contacts with J. Kropfgans and E. G. Baron, both well-known lutenists in Europe. While living in Cöthen Bach invented an instrument he called a *Lute-Clavicembalo*, a keyboard instrument meant to imitate the sound of a lute. This leads one to assume that much of Bach's lute music was meant for this instrument or that the instruments were interchangeable. In all the Suites, however, the writing is completely idiomatic to the lute. The Fourth Lute Suite and the Fuge in G minor are transcriptions from the solo violin partitas and the Third Lute Suite is a transcription from the solo cello suites. The remaining compositions were written exclusively for the lute.

In this edition I have tried to footnote every editorial change, with the exception of octave transposition and ornamentation. Octave transposition is shown $\begin{bmatrix} & \\ & _{(8)} \end{bmatrix}$. This indicates that it was written down an octave in the original.

I would suggest that one should use this book in conjunction with the *Bach-Gesellschaft* edition to realize any changes in ornamentation. All the phrase markings from the *Gesellschaft* have been kept intact. A dotted line indicates a left-hand slur and is always editorial.

Suite I

BWV 996

Passaggio

Allemande

Courante

Sarabande

Bouree

Gigue

14

Notes

Prelude

1.

2.

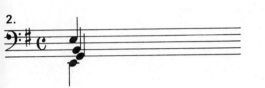

3.

4.

5.

6.

7.   In the original, this bass B is a whole note tied to the bass B in the following measure.

Presto

1. An alternate fingering:

2.

4.

3.

Allemande

1.

2.

3.

4.

5.

Courante

1.

2.

3.

Sarabande

1.

2.

3.

4.

5.

Gigue

1.

2.

3.

4.

5.

6.

7.

8.

9.

10.

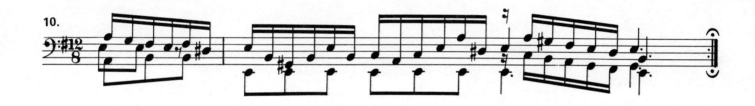

Suite II

BWV 997

Preludio

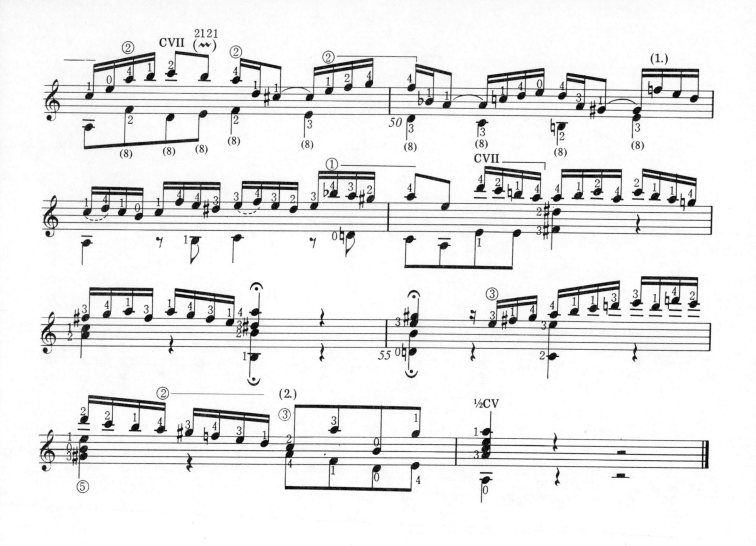

Fuga

*(also harmonic ⑥, 12th fret)

28

Sarabande

Gigue

Double

34

35

Notes

Preludio

1. From this point on (up to the double bar) the original is one octave lower.

Fuga

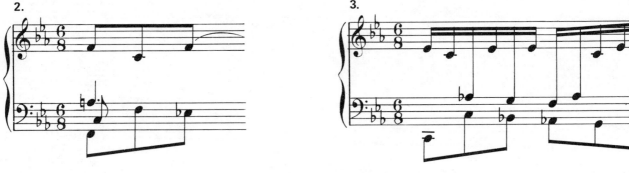

rabande

2.

uble

From this point up to the double bar, the original is one octave lower.

This measure is one octave lower in the original.

4.

5. From this point on, the original is one octave lower.

6.

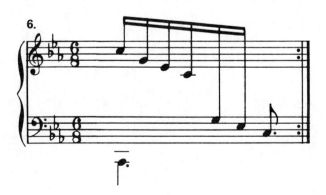

Suite III

BWV 995

Prelude

Presto

41

42

Allemande

Courante

Sarabande

Gavotte I

48

49

Gavotte II en rondeau

50

Da Capo Gavotte I al fine

Gigue

Notes

Presto

1.

3.

2.

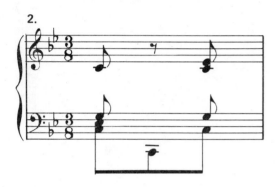

Allemande

1.

2.

Courante

1.

2.

3.

4.

5.

Gavotte I

1.

Gavotte II

1.

2.

Gigue

1.

2.

Suite IV

Prelude

BWV 1006a

55

57

59

60

Loure

Gavotte en rondeau

64

Menuet I

Menuet II

Da Capo Menuet I (al ⌒)

Bouree

Gigue

Notes

Prelude

1.

2.

3.

forte   *etc.*

4.

*(*f*)*   *etc.*

5.

etc.

72

Loure

1.

2.

etc.

Gavotte en rondeau

1.

2.

etc.

Menuet I

1.

Gigue

1.

2.

Prelude, Fuge, and Allegro

BWV 998

Fuge

80

Allegro

85

Notes

Fuge

Allegro

Prelude

BWV 999

87

Fuge

90

Notes

Fuge

6.

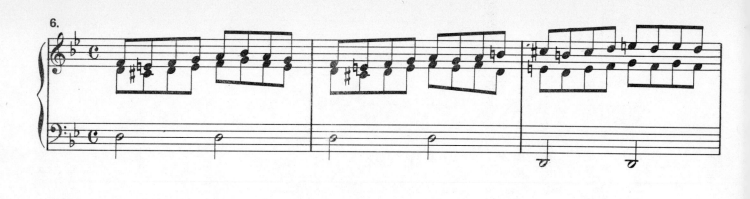

7.

8.

9.

10.